Reduce, Reuse, Recycle

Plastic

Alexandra Fix

Heinemann Library
Chicago, Illinois

© **2008 Heinemann Library**
an imprint of Capstone Global Library, LLC
Chicago, Illinois

Customer Service 888-454-2279
Visit our website at www.heinemannraintree.com

Designed by Steven Mead and Debbie Oatley
Printed in the United States of America in Eau Claire, Wisconsin.   052013   007384R

15 14 13
10 9 8 7 6 5 4 3

10-digit ISBNs: 1-4034-9716-8 (hc) 1-4034-9724-9 (pb)

Library of Congress Cataloging-in-Publication Data
Fix, Alexandra, 1950-
  Plastic / Alexandra Fix.
    p. cm. -- (Reduce, reuse, recycle)
  Includes bibliographical references and index.
  ISBN 978-1-4034-9716-1 (hc) -- ISBN 978-1-4034-9724-6 (pb)
  1. Plastic scrap--Recycling--Juvenile literature. I. Title.
  TD798.F55 2007
  668.4'192--dc22
                        2007002790

Acknowledgments
The author and publisher are grateful to the following for permission to reproduce copyright material: Alamy pp. **4** (Michael Klinec), **5** (Thorsten Indra), **8** (Lourens Smack), **12** (Mike Greenslade), **13** (David Ball), **15** (Manor Photography), **17** (Sébastien Baussais), **19** (Agripicture Images), **20** (Kim Karpeles), **22** (Photofusion Picture Library), **24** (David R. Frazier Photolibrary, Inc.); Corbis pp. **7** (Royalty Free), **10** (Alberto Esteves/EPA), **14** (Ariel Skelley), **23** (Master Photo Syndication/SYGMA), **25**, **27** (Bob Krist); Getty Images p. **21** (Digital Vision); Harcourt Education Ltd. pp. **6** (Ginny Stroud-Lewis), **16** (Ginny Stroud-Lewis), **26** (Ginny Stroud-Lewis); Science Photo Library pp. **9** (Philippe Spaila), **11** (George Lepp/Agstock), **18**.

Cover photograph reproduced with permission of Corbis/Randy Faris.

Every effort has been made to contact copyright holders of any material reproduced in this book. Any omissions will be rectified in subsequent printings if notice is given to the publisher.

Contents

Some words are shown in bold, **like this**. You can find out what they mean by looking in the glossary.

What Is Plastic Waste?

These plastic bottles have been saved for recycling.

People use plastic every day. Water bottles, sandwich bags, and food containers are common plastic items. Plastic is strong and can last a long time, but it is not easy to get rid of plastic.

Plastic waste is plastic that is thrown away. When plastic is buried in dirt, it is almost impossible to destroy. Many plastic items can be reused or **recycled**. This would waste less plastic.

These plastic bottles have been crushed and bundled. They are ready for recycling.

What Is Made of Plastic?

Many household items are made of plastic. There are plastic water bottles, milk bottles, trash bags and containers, storage bags, and hangers. Outdoor furniture such as chairs can also be made of plastic.

Many food items are packaged in plastic.

Some parts of race cars are made of plastic so the cars will be lighter and faster.

Many toys, balls, helmets, and games are made of plastic. Some clothes are made from plastic threads. Carpets, boats, **electronics**, and car parts can be made of plastic, too.

Where Does Plastic Come From?

Plastic is made from oil or natural gas found deep in the earth. Oil is mixed with **chemicals** and heated. This mixture becomes soft or liquid plastic.

These plastic pellets will be used to make a plastic item.

Hot liquid plastic is poured into a mold and cooled down to make these toy blocks.

Plastic is made in **factories**. It can be molded into shapes such as food containers or made into long threads to make larger items.

Will We Always Have Plastic?

Oil is dark in color.

Oil is the main ingredient in most plastic. Oil is a **nonrenewable resource**. If our oil supply gets used up, it will be gone forever.

Scientists are starting to use corn and natural sugars to make plastic. These materials are **renewable resources**. They also do not last as long as plastic made from oil.

Plastic made from corn oil is better for the **environment**.

What Happens When We Waste Plastic?

When plastic is thrown away, it is eventually brought to a **landfill**. In a landfill, plastic does not rot. It piles up higher and higher.

More than six million tons of litter are put into the ocean every year.

Landfills can release harmful gases into the air.

Throwing away plastic wastes **nonrenewable resources**. Garbage trucks that bring plastic to landfills run on **fuel**. The fuel comes from oil, a nonrenewable resource. The buried plastic is also made from oil.

How Can We Reduce Plastic Waste?

The best way to reduce plastic waste is to use less plastic. Try not to buy plastic things you do not need. Buy items with less plastic packaging.

Bring your own bag when you shop for food.

Throw-away food containers create a lot of plastic waste.

Pack your lunch in a reusable container instead of plastic wrap. Refill a sports bottle instead of buying bottled water. Do not use plastic silverware.

How Can We Reuse Plastic?

Plastic containers can be reused to store items.

You can rinse out and reuse plastic items, such as sandwich bags. Find new ways to use old plastic food containers. Decorate them and store your crayons, coins, or rock collection.

Give away plastic toys you no longer use. You could sell them at a garage sale in your neighborhood or give them to a store that sells used items.

Many toys are made of plastic.

How Can We Recycle Plastic?

When plastic is **recycled**, it is melted down and used again to make a new item. Most **communities** have a recycling program for plastic, paper, glass, and metal.

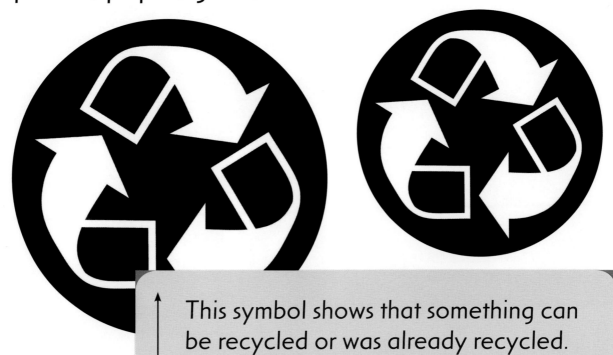

This symbol shows that something can be recycled or was already recycled.

Caps are made of plastic that is difficult to recycle.

After you have saved plastic items, get them ready for recycling. First wash and squash the used plastic containers and throw away plastic caps. You can leave labels on plastic bottles.

Where Can We Bring Plastic for Recycling?

Some places have **recycling** programs. People leave recycling bins outside their homes. A truck picks up the items and brings them to a recycling center.

Plastic, metal, and glass must be separated from paper in recycling bins.

Save plastic bottles until you can recycle them.

If your **community** does not have a recycling program, you can bring items to a recycling center or grocery store. From there they are taken to a **factory**, where they are melted down and made into recycled plastic.

How Is Plastic Recycled?

These flakes will be melted to make new plastic.

After plastic is brought to a **recycling** center, it is washed, sorted, and packed into large bundles. The bundles are chopped into tiny pieces called flakes.

The flakes are melted down and formed into spaghetti-like strands. Strands are cut into little pieces called pellets. Pellets are melted at **factories** to make new products.

This machine uses recycled plastic to make thin strands of plastic.

How Do We Use Recycled Plastic?

Recycled plastic can be used to make many things. Companies make carpets, trash bags, combs, and insulation out of recycled plastic.

It takes around 1,000 recycled plastic milk jugs to make a six-foot park bench.

This jacket is made of plastic fabric. →

Recycled plastic can even be used to make clothing, such as pants or the **fiberfill** stuffing in a warm jacket. Plastic can also be burned for **fuel** to make **electricity**.

How Can You Take Action?

You can help reduce, reuse, and **recycle** plastic. Ask your friends and family to start recycling plastic. You can help them get plastic items ready for recycling.

↑ Use leftover dishwater to rinse bottles for recycling.

Some communities have special days to remind people to recycle.

You can pick up plastic trash at school and in your neighborhood. Ask an adult to help you find where your **community's** recycling center is located. By reducing plastic waste, you can help keep our planet clean.

Search for the Recycle Symbol

Search for the **recycling** symbol on plastic products in your home and at school. Check if they have a number in the center.

Match that number to the chart on the next page. Check which types of plastic your **community** recycles. Some recycling centers will only take number one and number two plastic.

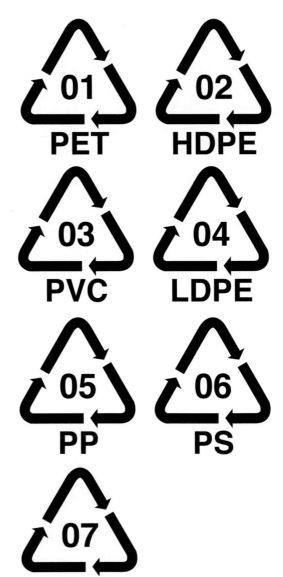

1	PET	two-liter beverage bottles, mouthwash bottles
2	HDPE	milk jugs, trash bags, detergent bottles
3	PVC	cooking oil bottles, packaging around meat
4	LDPE	grocery bags, produce bags, food wrap, bread bags
5	PP	yogurt containers, shampoo bottles, straws, margarine tubs, diapers
6	PS	hot beverage cups, take-out boxes, egg cartons, meat trays, CD cases
7	Other	all other types of plastic or packaging made from more than one type of plastic

Glossary

chemical	basic element that makes up all things
community	group of people who live in an area
electricity	form of energy that can be used to create light, heat, and power
electronics	items such as radios, televisions, and computers that use electricity
environment	natural surroundings for people, animals, and plants
factory	building or buildings where something is produced
fiberfill	warm stuffing made from plastic that is used in jackets
fuel	something that is burned for power or heat
landfill	large area where trash is dumped, crushed, and covered with soil
nonrenewable resource	material of the earth that cannot be replaced by nature
recycle	break down a material and use it again to make a new product. Recycling is the act of breaking down a material and using it again.
renewable resource	material of the earth that can be replaced

Find Out More

Books to Read

Galko, Francine. *Earth Friends at the Grocery Store*. Chicago: Heinemann Library, 2004.

Lucas, Rhonda Donald. *Plastic*. Mankato, MN: Capstone Press, 2004.

Oxlade, Chris. *How We Use Plastic*. Chicago: Raintree, 2004.

Web Sites

The Environmental Protection Agency works to protect the air, water, and land. The organization has a special Web site for students at <u>www.epa.gov/kids</u>.

Earth911 is an organization that gives information about where you can recycle in your community. Their Web site for students is <u>http://www.earth911.org/master.asp?s=kids&a=kids/kids.asp</u>.

Index